MAKING SENSE OF
LITERACY ASSESSMENTS

A RUNNING RECORDS WORKBOOK

TARA WILSON Ed.D.

SECOND EDITION

Kendall Hunt
publishing company

Cover image © Shutterstock.com
All images are created by Tara Wilson unless otherwise credited.

Kendall Hunt
p u b l i s h i n g c o m p a n y

www.kendallhunt.com
Send all inquiries to:
4050 Westmark Drive
Dubuque, IA 52004-1840

Copyright © 2019, 2021 by Kendall Hunt Publishing Company

Pak ISBN: 978-17924-5110-2
Textbook ISBN: 978-1-7924-2485-4

Published in the United States of America

Contents

Introduction

Welcome!

Dear student,

This is not another expensive textbook that you will return to the bookstore; you're holding in your hand a workbook that is yours! This book will serve as a valuable resource not just for a semester but even after you finish your educator preparation program.

This workbook will help you make sense of the literacy assessments, specifically running records that you will administer to countless young scholars. Please read onto the next page to learn more about your workbook!

Sincerely,
Dr. Wilson

How to Use This Workbook

Purpose

The purpose of this teacher (preservice and practicing) workbook is to serve not only as a resource but also as a place to practice running records. This workbook is intended to help you understand the literacy assessments better in a to-the-point type style. Therefore, this workbook is divided into five practical sections, as well as blank pages at the back to take notes.

Section 1: Assessments 101 will provide you with important background information on literacy assessments. The topics included in this section are purposes of assessments, student involvement, and different types thereof.

Section 2: Running Records will focus solely on running records. Different aspects of a running record are explained. These aspects are coding, advantages, administering, analysis, and types of errors. There is a statement of caution in Section 2. Do not be frightened, it is there to serve as words of wisdom.

Section 3: Selections give you several short stories for practice. You will use these original (written by graduate students and myself) stories to practice conducting running records. The selections are preceded by a brief explanation of how to conduct these running records.

Section 4: Reading Difficulties will provide you with signs of possible reading difficulties. Dyslexia will also be discussed in this section.

Section 5: Resources provides a plethora of information for further exploration and continued learning about literacy assessments.

Features

- Spiral bound—easier to fold the book back, without creating any extra wear and tear
- Perforated pages—you never know if you are going to want to remove a page and put it somewhere else
- Blank note space—room to write notes from class lectures, professional developments, thoughts, etc.
- Practice stories—no need to go looking for appropriate stories to use for running records
- Reflection opportunities—many places to write your reflections down
- Easy-to-use format—allows you to quickly access the information you want

Assessments 101

Source: Tara Wilson

Introduction

Conducting assessments is unavoidable and is probably the most dreaded part of a teacher's day. Luckily, an assessment does not always mean a pen-and-paper standardized test. A variety of assessment options are available. It is vital that every teacher has, at minimum, a novice level of assessment knowledge in order to utilize all assessments efficiently. Chappuis et al. (2012) refer to this knowledge as *classroom assessment literacy* (see Figure 1.1). Fortunately, most teachers' wheelhouses encompass a considerable amount of assessment knowledge because assessments have always been a part of high-quality teaching.

This section will cover three aspects of assessments: purpose, student involvement, and types.

FIGURE 1.1

> Classroom assessment literacy—the ability to collect accurate information and to use the data in an effective way to improve student achievement.

Table 1.1	
Aspect	**Examples**
Content	Using spelling lists at varying readiness levels of students Providing reading materials at varying readability levels
Process	Using tiered activities through which students work with the same understandings and skills but move about it with different levels of support Offering manipulatives or other hands-on supports
Product	Giving students options on how to demonstrate learning Allowing students to work alone, in pairs or in small groups
Environment	Providing places in the room to work quietly, without distractions, and areas that encourage student collaboration Establishing routines that allow students to receive help when the teacher cannot help them immediately

Purpose

Why are assessments so important? What purpose do they serve? In a nutshell, assessments provide specific, pertinent information. In the terms of literacy, McKenna and Stahl (2015) proclaim, "assessment is the first step in addressing the most urgent needs of our developing readers" (p. 2). Outcomes of any assessment ought to be effectively conveyed in a timely and comprehensible manner. The information provided by assessments guides teachers, administers, parents, and even students as they make educational decisions.

Teachers use information from assessments to support and verify their students' learning. One popular delivery mode of information is via differentiated instruction. Differentiated instruction occurs when a teacher customizes his or her instruction to meet the diverse needs of their learners. There are four aspects of a lesson that a teacher can differentiate: content (i.e., what a student needs to learn), process (i.e., educational activities the student engages in), product (culminating project that illustrates what the student learned), or environment (the way a classroom feels and operates). Refer to Table 1.1 for examples on how to differentiate each aspect.

Regardless of what aspect a teacher chooses to differentiate, the use of continuing assessment makes differentiated instruction an effective approach to learning.

To tell what each student needs, assessments provide information on what a student has or has not yet learned. When two or more students score the same on an assessment, it is important to note what part(s) the students struggled with *and* for what reason. This information assists teachers with choosing what kind of instructional intervention is needed. Teachers can target their instruction to put the student back on track to proficiency. Thus, assessments guide teachers as they plan for their implantation of differentiated instruction.

When implemented correctly, assessments can provide valuable information on a district's or school's reading program(s). Campus administrators use information from assessments to measure student achievement. The data on student achievement assist administrators when making key judgments, that is, whether to continue a program due to its effectiveness or decisions on what to do about increasing student competence. District administrators learn about the overall effectiveness of their reading curriculum and how well each school performs in literacy.

Parents use information from assessments to see what kind of progress their child is making. The data helps parents to decide if they should arrange to meet with the teacher, to seek tutoring options, to feel comfortable about where their child is at, etc.

As for students, they use information from assessments as opportunities to illustrate their understanding. More on students and their involvement in assessments follows next.

FIGURE 1.2

> Students must be *trained* in self-assessment so that they realize the purposes of their learning, thus grasping what they need to achieve.
> This does not come naturally!

Benefits of Student Involvement

Assessments are not only beneficial for teachers, administrators, and parents but also for students. This might be a shift in thinking for those who view students as testees. Students, when involved in the assessment process, benefit greatly. But what are those benefits? And how can students be involved?

Who does not achieve more when they are given ownership over the learning process? Assessments allow students to self-assess, to set achievable goals, to track progress, and to reflect on and share their learning with others. For a word of caution, see Figure 1.2.

When data from assessments are shared with students, then students become active users of assessments. However, this means more than just handing a graded test back. Teachers should confer with each student to discuss an assessment. The conversation between the teacher and the student must be contemplative, considerate, and focused to explore understanding, and must be led so that both parties receive opportunities to express their thinking or ideas.

Teachers also need to assist students in creating academic goals. Students should be able to identify their strengths, weaknesses, and areas for further study. Data binders are a great way for *any* student to organize their learning. Visit the resource section at the back of your workbook for more information on data binders.

But, shouldn't students be involved with assessments *before* they are actually given? Yes! Chappuis (2012) asserts, "We know that students' chances of success improve when they start out with a vision of where they are headed." The notion of students having a voice in the total assessment process correlates with the fact that students' motivation increases, and learning is more effective, when students are active in their own education.

At the end of the day, the student is the one who decides whether they believe they can achieve their goal(s) or not. They are the ones who decide to keep or quit working toward their goal. The teacher's instruction will benefit the student's learning only if the student decides to keep working. With that said, in regard to assessment, teachers must keep their students aware of their progress in a way that students will keep trying and believing in themselves.

Types

As evidenced earlier, transparency is key to understanding assessments. Another important aspect of assessments is knowing that there are two distinct types: formative and summative. Formative assessments provide information about a student's progress towards a goal, whereas summative assessments are given at the end of a unit and or grading period, they reveal how well the student mastered an objective. These types involve both conventional tests and less structured methods of gathering data. A list characterizing each type is given here.

© Africa Studio/Shutterstock.com

Formative assessments:

- For practice
- For learning (to support and to improve)
- During instruction
- For gathering evidence
- Sometimes for a grade
- Inform what should come next in learning
- Identify what standards students are struggling with
- Assist in diagnosing student needs
- Are a collection of practices
- Inform instruction
- Provide descriptive feedback learners need to grow

What are some examples?

Summative assessments:

- Count toward a grade
- Of learning
- Occur periodically
- Identify what standards each student has mastered
- After instruction
- Determine the level of student achievement
- Provide evidence of achievement
- Verify learning
- Report what learning has already occurred
- Let all recipients understand the sufficiency of student learning
- Reflect achievement at a point in time

© progressman/Shutterstock.com

What are some examples?

It is important to note that "establishing a balance between formative and summative uses at the classroom level is the most significant contributor to increased student achievement" (Chappuis, 2012).

Review

What do you feel are three big takeaways from this section?

1.

2.

3.

Draw a double bubble or a Venn diagram representing formative and summative assessments.

Thoughts to Ponder

Reflect on each of the following statements and questions. Write your reflection in the space provided. Then discuss your thoughts with a partner.

"They say what gets measured gets done."

"I used to think of assessment as an ending to a learning event."

What type of assessment are running records?

Do you self-assess? If so, how? If not, why?

Running Records

Source: Tara Wilson

Introduction

Running records are coded remarks of a student's reading of text. Running records illustrate how well a student can read (i.e. number of words read correctly) and their reading behaviors (what they say and do as they read). A teacher catches a glimpse of how a student does or does not utilize various reading strategies.

A teacher notes everything a student says as they read a selection, including all words read correctly and incorrectly (Reutzel & Cooter, 2019). Running records supply data for documenting a student's progress. Running records are used as an instrument for error analysis. After a teacher codes a student's reading, all errors are evaluated. This evaluation will determine the type(s) of or reason(s) for errors. After analyzing the running records, a teacher will be better equipped to strengthen a student's reading ability.

Don't worry; like anything else it takes practice and time to become comfortable with this process. With each running record created on a student, the teacher's coding ability gets refined.

Advantages of Running Records

All running records come with two main advantages: flexibility and ease of administration. One example of flexibility is that the length of text is not dictated, but a suggested length is 100 to 200 words. This length allows teachers to use a variety of texts for running records.

Another example of flexibility is that any text, not just prepared text, can generate running records. Authentic texts are normally used. Clay (2013) advises running records to be administered using *any* texts that a student can read with at least 90% accuracy. Leveled books that contain a complete story or informational text are used mostly for benchmark texts for systematic assessment and not for the normal running record.

An example of ease of administration is that a running record can be conducted more often than an informal reading inventory (IRI) or even a miscue analysis. Running records have the adaptability to be given in a more authentic setting where a variety of texts are available. They give teachers the ability to closely observe how a particular student approaches text.

Informal Reading Inventory

An IRI is an exam that is often given individually to students (though some can be administered to a small group). According to Reutzel and Cooter (2019), the IRI "is one of the best tools for observing and analyzing reading performance and for gathering information about how a student uses a wide range of reading strategies" (p 423). Teachers are able to obtain a good estimate of a student's ability on leveled reading materials. Not only that, but often times IRIs can provide data on other key reading areas such as fluency, comprehension and word identification (via a running record). These inventories are considered informal because most of the time they do not provide norms, reliability or validity information. Teachers can create their own IRIs by simply using reading material they have in their classroom. However, commercially IRIs are available, for example the popular Developmental Reading Assessment (DRA).

Administering a Running Record

For the most part, every running record follows the same process. First, you choose a book or selection that is near the student's reading level. If the text chosen is too easy or too hard, then simply chose another text.

Right before starting a running record, you should inform the student that you will be writing some notes as the student reads a selection aloud. Some students will worry and focus more on what you are writing. Try to make the student feel at ease.

The selection ought to be unfamiliar to the student, so it is imperative that you tell a very brief introduction (one or two sentences) to the story before the student starts to read.

During the reading, you will be very busy recording and observing. You should use a typed paper with the same words the student is reading (see section 3). Put little checkmarks or slashes above or next to each word that is read correctly and mark errors (see "coding" later on in this section). Try not to intervene while the student is reading. You do not want to disrupt them and plus, you are trying to see what they can do without assistance. Notice if and how the student uses strategies that were taught in class.

After the student is finished reading, ask them to retell the story and some comprehension questions (see section 3 for examples). Write down their responses. Then confer with the student about their performance. Praise them for any self-corrections made and / or strategies used. Give feedback in a constructive manner.

Analyzing a Running Record

After conducting a running record, analysis occurs by analyzing a running record, the teacher obtains a view of their student's involvement in the reading process rather than a product evaluation that standardized reading tests offer.

Table 2.1	Woods and Moe (2015) Reading Levels	
Level	**Accuracy**	**Comprehension**
Independent	99%–100%	90%–100%
Definite Instructional	95%–98%	75%–89%
Transitional Instructional	91%–94%	51%–74%
Frustration	90% and below	50% and below

It is also important for a teacher to record interpretations and any observations somewhere on the running record sheet. This information will prove to be valuable later when the teacher is analyzing the codes. Student behaviors apparent in running records should guide lesson planning and on-the-spot teaching decisions.

One important piece of information that a running record provides is the student's accuracy rate (See Table 2.1). The teacher can discover the reading skills of the student. There are three levels of accuracy rates: independent, instructional, and frustration. To find out the accuracy rate, take the ratio of errors to running words, like this E/RW. Clay (2000) advises that ratios under 1:10 allow for the greatest opportunities to observe students interacting with text. Usually, if a student's error ratio is low, then the student is capable of using different types of information to self-monitor. If a student has an error ratio over 1:9 with a text selection, then the student might be discouraged to show their usual reading processes. A higher ratio might mean that the student is ignoring information that can be useful in monitoring and adjusting reading. Another way of calculating a student's accuracy rate is by using this formula: (number of words in the selection minus number of uncorrected mistakes) times 100 divided by the number of words in the selection. For example: (116 words – 8 errors) × 100/116 = 93%.

An additional piece of information provided by a running record is a self-correction ratio. This ratio reveals to which degree a student is monitoring their reading or using different cueing systems to read. To find this number, take the ratio of self-corrections to the total number of errors and self-corrections, the formula is SC/E + SC.

Coding

A main purpose of coding a running record is to let the teacher have a record he or she can "play back" later. These records do not have to be made on preprinted sheets. Teachers can code a reading on any sheet of blank paper or an index card. A teacher does not have time to analyze and reflect on how a student is doing while he or she is conducting a running record. Thus, it is important to use rememberable and meaningful codes. How does a teacher know what codes to use and when?

Unfortunately, or fortunately (depends on how you look at it), a variety of codes exist. This is because there is not a consensus on how or which miscues should be coded. One example is provided here. More examples of codes are provided later in this workbook. However, ultimately, which codes a teacher uses matters very little if two rules are followed: (1) the teacher stays consistent, and (2) others must be familiar with whatever system is used when coded selections are shared.

The selection *Big* by Tara Wilson (2019) is used to show a coding system.

1. Words read correctly should be marked with a slash. Lines of slashes need to correspond to lines of text. The solid line indicates a page break.

I will be big when I grow up said Nel	/ / / / / / / / / /
My arms will grow	/ / / /
My feet will grow	/ / / /
My head will grow too	/ / / / /

2. To show an incorrect response, write what was said over it.

I will be big when I grow up said Nel	/ / / / / / / / / $\frac{\text{Ned}}{\text{Nel}}$
My arms will grow	$\frac{\text{Me}}{\text{My}}$ / / /
My feet will grow	/ / / /
My head will grow too	/ $\frac{\text{heart}}{\text{head}}$ / / /

3. Put an X to record an omission.

I will be big when I grow up said Nel	/ / / / / / / / x x
My arms will grow	x / / /
My feet will grow	x / / /
My head will grow too	x / / / x

4. Document an insertion by writing the word and putting a dash under it.

I will be big when I grow up said Nel	/ / / <u>very</u> / / / / / /
My arms will grow	/ / /
My feet will grow	/ / / <u>too</u>
My head will grow too	/ / / / /

5. To mark a self-correction, write *SC* next to the word they said first. *SC* should not be recorded as errors.

I will be big when I grow up said Nel	/ / / / / / / / / $\frac{\text{Ned SC}}{\text{Nel}}$
My arms will grow	/ / / $\frac{\text{grew SC}}{\text{Grow}}$
My feet will grow	/ / / /
My head will grow too	/ / / / /

6. Write an *R* by any word that is repeated. Repetitions should not be recorded as errors.

I will be big when I grow up said Nel	/ / / big R / / / / / /
My arms will grow	/ / / grow R
My feet will grow	/ / / grow R
My head will grow too	/ / / / /

7. If a student takes longer than 5 seconds to say a word, and the teacher decides to tell the student the word, then put a T (for told) next to the word. This *should* be recorded as an error.

I will be big when I grow up said Nel	/ / / / / / grow T / said /
My arms will grow	/ / / /
My feet will grow	/ / / /
My head will grow too	/ / / / too

Miscue Analysis

After analyzing a running record, it is imperative for the teacher to dive a little deeper and conduct a miscue analysis, which can be completed on a separate worksheet. A miscue analysis provides a view of how a student processes text and their use of strategies (Serravallo, 2018). The teacher analyzes the oral errors a student made while reading and draws conclusions about what strategies the student used or did not use to decode words. With a running record, the teacher basically just noted errors. But what kind of errors did the student make, and how can that information guide instruction?

Three Types of Errors

The letters M, S, and V will be the most important letters when conducting a miscue analysis. It is important to note that word identification depends on three types of cues. Each time a student makes an error, the teacher should write one of those letters over in the error column. (See Table 2.2) What do the letters stand for? What information do they provide? (See Table 2.3)

You Give it a Try in Section 3!

Table 2.2	Types of Cues				
Term	**Abbreviation**	**Meaning**	**Definition**	**Question to Ask**	**Example**
Semantic	M	Meaning	Attempt at making sense, the substitution fits the meaning of the story	Does it make sense?	(text) *alligator* (student) *gator*
Syntax	S	Structure	Uses rules of oral language, sentence can be read that way up to substitution and sound right	Does it sound right?	(text) *he* (student) *him*
Graphophonic	V	Visual	Shares some of the same letters	Does it look right?	(text) *pay* (student) *play*

Table 2.3	Sample Miscue Analysis							
Text	**Student**		**V**			**S**	**M**	**SC?**
		B	M	E			
outside	out	/			/	/	
her	here	/	/		/		/
under	your				/		
puppy	dog				/	/	

Table 2.4	Major Types of Miscues		
Type	**Definition**	**Example**	**Your Example**
Omission	A skipped word	The ~~little~~ girl	
Insertion	Added word or phrase	The (big) dog	
Substitution	Replaced word for another	Kitten—cat	
Reversal	Changing the order	Saw—was	
Teacher-supplied word	Long hesitation so the teacher pronounces the word	. . . . . .—cactus	
Repetition	Repeats a word or phrase	Shrimp, shrimp	
Ignoring punctuation	Disregards periods, commas, exclamation points, etc.	I am hungry!	
Hesitation	Break, but not long enough for the teacher to provide	. . . chef	
Self-correction	Rereads one or more words to correct an error	Go gone, gone	

Keep it Organized!

Doing running records is a lot of work, especially if there are a lot of students in the classroom. By being organized, a teacher can reduce their stress (even if just a little). Here are three tips:

Make a schedule. Designate each student a day of the week or month (depending on how frequently you plan on conducting running records and how many students you have) that they will be assess. This will ensure that every student will have a running record that is updated on a regular basis.

Maintain a data binder (see section 5) on each student. Have a section in this binder to store all of their running records. This section will illustrate progress the student has made (i.e. Reading at a higher level with increased accuracy, well hopefully).

Decide on a goal with each student. This goal should be centered on a particular reading behavior that will help the student advance to the next level. While conferring with the student, always go back to the goal.

Statements of Caution

There are a few words of wisdom or statements of caution (depending on what lens is used) a teacher needs to keep in mind when analyzing running records and student responses to any questions that may be asked.

Miscues

- A recurring issue most teachers experience is deciding which miscues to actually tally. How a teacher handles this issue can alter a student's running record results, thus leading to a different conclusion about whether a particular selection is on the student's independent, instructional, or frustration level. Teachers must ask themselves, "Can a particular miscue be left out when figuring out the total?" The most common type of errors that teachers struggle with include ignoring punctuation, hesitations, insertions, reversals, omissions, repetitions, teacher-supplied words, and substitutions (Table 2.4). The best advice, as mentioned previously, is to stay consistent and, of course, follow what the particular school district says.

Reading a-z Running Record

Level D

Student's Name ___Matt Jones___   Date ___1/28/02___

**The Wheel
99 words**

Have the student read out loud as you record.   Assessed by ___B. Castillo___

page	E = errors S-C = self-correction M = meaning S = structure V = visual	E	S-C	E M S V	S-C M S V
3	✓ ✓ ✓ of/sc ✓ ✓ The wheel comes off the truck.		1	M S Ⓥ	Ⓜ Ⓢ V
4	✓ ✓ ✓ ✓ It rolls down the hill. ✓ ✓ ✓ Faster and faster.				
5	✓ ✓ went/goes ✓ ✓ ✓ The wheel rolls through the field. ✓ ✓ p/✓ — ✓ It rolls past the cows. ✓R ✓ ✓ Faster and faster.	1 1		Ⓜ Ⓢ V	
6	✓ ✓ ✓ ✓ farm The wheel rolls through the barn. ✓ ✓ TA It rolls [past the chickens.] ✓ ✓ Faster and faster.	1 1		Ⓜ Ⓢ V M S V	
7	✓ ✓ ✓ ✓R₂ ✓ water The wheel rolls toward the river. ✓ ✓ ✓ ✓ T It rolls over the bridge. ✓ ✓ ✓ Faster and faster.	1 1		Ⓜ Ⓢ V M S V	
8	✓ ✓ ✓ in/sc ✓ ✓ The wheel rolls into the school. ✓ ✓ ✓ of ✓ ✓ It rolls out∧the door. ✓ ✓ ✓ Faster and faster. ✓ ✓ ✓ ⌐ ─R The wheel rolls✓through the town.	1	1	M Ⓢ V	M S Ⓥ
9	✓ ✓ ✓ P/✓ R It rolls past the policeman. ✓ ✓ ✓ Faster and faster.				
10	✓ ✓ ✓ ✓ ✓ T The wheel rolls into the garage. ✓ ✓ ✓ It stops rolling. ✓ ✓ ✓ ✓ ✓ track/sc The wheel is on the truck.	1	1	M S V M S Ⓥ	Ⓜ Ⓢ V
	Totals	8	3		

Accuracy Rate: **91%**   Error Rate: **1:11**   Self-correction Rate: **1:4**

- Semantical (meaning) miscues can effect a student's reading level. Sometimes it is acceptable to consider deviations from the text, and sometimes these errors should not be counted. McKenna and Stahl (2015) point out that the "Qualitative Reading Inventory—5 (Leslie & Caldwell, 2010), provides two ways of determining the instructional level: (1) counting all miscues and (2) counting only those that significantly change the meaning of the text" (p. 66).

- When a student uses one word for another, that is, a substitution miscue, it should *not* be seen as an error *if* the new word is similar in meaning (e.g., puppy for dog). The teacher still needs to note that the student has used semantic and syntactic cues.

- Teachers hope that students will monitor their own reading, and when a miscue does not fit, teachers assume that the student will notice and try to correct it. However, if a student does not try to fix it, then the student is not monitoring their reading for sense.

Questions

- When possible, conduct a pretest to determine prior knowledge. It is recommended for teachers to give selections on familiar and unfamiliar topics, and then compare the student's responses.

- When answering comprehension questions, students may respond correctly due to background knowledge instead of what they just read. This is especially true when the questions are inferential in nature (McKenna & Stahl, 2015). Thus, teachers should be guarded when interpreting the results from selections on familiar topics.

- Not all questions are created equal, and this affects assessing comprehension. How a student performs depends on the difficulty level of the questions asked; some are easy, and some are more challenging. The questions a teacher asks may result in a different decision on whether a particular selection is on the student's independent, instructional, or frustration level.

Review

What do you feel are three big takeaways from this section?

1.

2.

3.

Thoughts to Ponder

Reflect on each of the following statements and questions. Write your reflection in the space provided. Then discuss your thoughts with a partner.

How do we ensure inter-tester reliability on a campus?

Is there important information in the patterns of miscues? Why, or why not?

Why should a teacher conduct running records? Serravallo (2017) conducted a study on comprehension with 4th grade students. She found "when looking at whole-book comprehension, students typically demonstrated strong comprehension in books about two levels lower than a short-passage running record indicated" (p 5). What do you think that is?

The assignment for this section is to complete a running record. Use section 3.

Selections

Source: Tara Wilson

There are 10 selections in this section. They are for students in grades kindergarten through third grade. Feel free to make copies of any of the selections. You are to use these to practice running records. The copy that states "student version" is given to the student and you use the copy that states "teacher version" to write notes, observations, and so on.

Steps for Giving Each Selection

*Please note that you may skip over, repeat, and/or alter any of the following steps if in your "professional" opinion; particular situations seem to permit it.

1. Read the selection to yourself first, checking for any words that might be a problem.

2. Ask the student question(s) that tap into their prior knowledge or identify the topic.

3. Have the student read the selection aloud to you. You may remind them to read carefully because they might be asked questions or to retell once they have finished.

4. As the student reads, code miscues. If the student hesitates too long (about 6 seconds), tell them the word, but remember to note it on your sheet.

    *Stop the student if (a) the selection is so difficult that you feel it could be labeled at the "frustration" level, or (b) you have had to tell the student too many words.

5. When the student completes a selection, ask some comprehension questions (read note at the bottom of this page).

6. Use scoring guidelines (discussed in Section 2) to determine the level of the selection read. Decide on an overall judgment as to whether the selection is frustration, instructional, or independent. Caution: This is not always clear-cut.

*Note: Some comprehension questions are provided for the selections in this workbook. However, you are encouraged to practice your questioning skills by developing your own questions. ☺

Big

Written by Tara Wilson
43 words, Kindergarten
Student Version

"I will be big when I grow up!" said Nel. My arms will grow. My feet will grow. My head will grow, too. What if my nose does not get big? My nose will be a baby nose on a big face! Funny!"

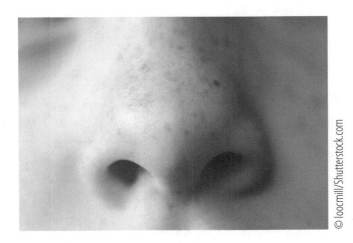

© loocmill/Shutterstock.com

Big

Written by Tara Wilson
43 words, Kindergarten
Teacher Version

"I will be big when I grow up!" said Nel. My arms will grow. My feet will grow. My head will grow, too. What if

my nose does not get big? My nose will be a baby nose on a big face! Funny!"

_____ self-corrections _____ errors   types of miscues _____ (m) _____ (s) _____ (v)

Observations: Possible comprehension question: What is this about?

Josie and the Tattlers

Written by Lisa Brashier
220 words, 3rd grade
Student Version

Josie was a 2nd grader who always tried really hard to please her teacher and friends. She tried her best to be a good student and make good grades. Unfortunately, though, Josie hung out with friends who were known as "tattle-tales" which are people who constantly tattle on others and sometimes even make it seem worse than it really is. Every time Josie turned around, one of her friends was tattling to the teacher. Josie found it annoying that her friends were like this, so much so that one day she decided she wanted to teach her friends a lesson. She talked to her teacher about how her friends were behaving and asked her teacher if she would play along with the idea. Josie's teacher agreed. She made it seem like her friends did a horrible thing and she "tattled" on them even though the teacher knew that Josie's friends had not done anything wrong. The teacher called all of Josie's friends to a meeting because they were all upset with Josie. She had Josie come in and talk to them about how they felt and told them that is how every other person feels when they tattle on them. Her friends apologized and decided to make a change and from then on they never tattled on anyone else again.

© Photographee.eu/Shutterstock.com

Josie and the Tattlers

Written by Lisa Brashier
220 words, 3rd grade
Teacher Version

Josie was a 2nd grader who always tried really hard to please her teacher and friends. She tried her best to be a good student and make good grades. Unfortunately, though, Josie hung out with friends who were known as "tattle-tales" which are people who constantly tattle on others and sometimes even make it seem worse than it really is. Every time Josie turned around, one of her friends was tattling to the teacher. Josie found it annoying that her friends were like this, so much so that one day she decided she wanted to teach her friends a lesson.

She talked to her teacher about how her friends were behaving and asked her teacher if she would play along with the idea. Josie's teacher agreed. She made it seem like her friends did a horrible thing and she "tattled" on them even though the teacher knew that Josie's friends had not done anything wrong. The teacher called all of Josie's friends to a meeting because they were all upset with Josie. She had Josie come in and talk to them about how they felt and told them that is how every other person feels when they tattle on them. Her friends apologized and decided to make a change and from then on they never tattled on anyone else again.

_3_ self-corrections   _2_ errors   types of miscues _1_ (m) _2_ (s) _0_ (v)

Observations: Possible comprehension question: What kind of friends did Josie have?

Bad ones. Friends that did not have each others back.

Pets

Written by Tara Wilson
70 words, 1st grade
Student Version

One day I found a duck. I took her home to live with me. The next day, my friend gave me a turtle, and I took it home. My mom was getting mad about my new pets. Then I found a lost rabbit and took it home, too. On another day, I saw a sad cow, so I took him home.

"No, not a cow! No more pets," Mom yelled.

Pets

Written by Tara Wilson
70 words, 1st grade
Teacher Version

One day I found a duck. I took her home to live with me. The next day, my friend gave me a turtle, and I took

it home. My mom was getting mad about my new pets. Then I found a lost rabbit and took it home, too. On

another day, I saw a sad cow, so I took him home.

  "No, not a cow! No more pets," Mom yelled.

_____ self-corrections _____ errors   types of miscues _____ (m) _____ (s) _____ (v)

Observations: Possible comprehension questions:

1) What kind of animals did the kid take home?

2) How did the mom feel about the cow?

Summer Day

Written by Tara Wilson
130 words, 1st grade
Student Version

It was a hot summer day. Mary and Sara were watching TV. Dad told them to turn the TV off.

"Go outside," he said. "Kids need to run and play."

Mary and Sara felt tired. The girls just wanted to sit.

"You two cannot just sit around all day. Go outside!" said Dad.

The two girls picked up a big ball and went outside. They threw the ball back and forth. Some kids across the road saw the girls.

"May we play, too?" the kids yelled.

"Ok," said Sara.

A little later, Dad went outside with some juice and smiled. "Being outside with friends is a good way to spend a summer day," said Dad.

The kids all agreed. It was more fun to play than sit around the house!

© 2xSamara.com/Shutterstock.com

Summer Day

Written by Tara Wilson
130 words, 1st grade
Teacher Version

It was a hot summer day. Mary and Sara were watching TV. Dad told them to turn the TV off.

"Go outside," he said. "Kids need to run and play."

Mary and Sara felt tired. The girls just wanted to sit.

"You two cannot just sit around all day. Go outside!" said Dad.

The two girls picked up a big ball and went outside. They threw the ball back and forth. Some kids across the road saw the girls.

"May we play, too?" the kids yelled.

"Ok," said Sara.

A little later, Dad went outside with some juice and smiled. "Being outside with friends is a good way to spend a summer day," said Dad.

The kids all agreed. It was more fun to play than sit around the house!

_____ self-corrections _____ errors   types of miscues _____ (m) _____ (s) _____ (v)

Observations: Possible comprehension questions:

1) Why did the girls go outside?

2) How did Dad feel about the girls watching TV?

The Lost Toy

Written by Tara Wilson
40 words, Kindergarten
Student Version

"I lost my toy," said the girl. "Can you help me find it?"

"I see it," said Big Sister. "I see it under your bed." "Do not worry, I will get it for you."

"I love you," said the girl.

© kryzhov/Shutterstock.com

The Lost Toy

Written by Tara Wilson
40 words, Kindergarten
Teacher Version

"I lost my toy," said the girl. "Can you help me find it?"

"I see it," said Big Sister. "I see it under your bed." "Do not worry, I will get it for you."

"I love you," said the girl.

_____ self-corrections _____ errors   types of miscues _____ (m) _____ (s) _____ (v)

Observations: Possible comprehension question: Where was the toy?

The Pond

Written by Tara Wilson
75 words, 1st grade
Student Version

Bob and Ted like going to the pond. Mom likes the pond, too. Bob fed the ducks. Ted saw a green frog.

Mom said, "Look at the red bird."

"I see a brown fish," said Ted. "Can we jump in the water?" asked the boys.

"No," said Mom, "Dad said we cannot get wet."

"But, Mom, it is hot," said Bob.

"Yes, it is," said Mom. She jumped in. In went Ted. In went Bob.

© ONYXprj/Shutterstock.com

The Pond

Written by Tara Wilson
75 words, 1st grade
Teacher Version

Bob and Ted like going to the pond. Mom likes the pond, too. Bob fed the ducks. Ted saw a green frog.

Mom said, "Look at the red bird."

"I see a brown fish," said Ted. "Can we jump in the water?" asked the boys.

"No," said Mom, "Dad said we cannot get wet."

"But, Mom, it is hot," said Bob.

"Yes, it is," said Mom. She jumped in. In went Ted. In went Bob.

_____ self-corrections _____ errors   types of miscues _____ (m) _____ (s) _____ (v)

Observations: Possible comprehension question: Why did Mom and the boys jump in the pond?

The Secret Mission

Written by Lisa Brashier
192 words, 4th grade
Student Version

Millie's mission was a risky one, as usual. She had spent the last 6 months in the jungles of the Amazon. She was searching for a long-lost relic that could be key to discovering a cure for many diseases. There was a tribe of people who live in the jungles of the Amazon that did not want this relic to be found because it was sacred to them. That is why the assignment was such a dangerous one. After a long and treacherous journey into the deep jungle, Millie was able to locate the relic and made a deal with the tribe in exchange for them allowing her to take the relic home with her. She explained how the relic could be helpful in curing millions of people and promised to handle it with care and respect. In exchange for food and supplies, the chief of the tribe agreed to allow Millie to take the relic. She returned home after an exhausting yet rewarding 6 months. She felt accomplished because she had successfully completed her mission and was hopeful that a cure for cancer was in the process of now being found.

The Secret Mission

Written by Lisa Brashier
192 words, 4th grade
Teacher Version

Millie's mission was a risky one, as usual. She had spent the last 6 months in the jungles of the Amazon. She was searching for a long-lost relic that could be key to discovering a cure for many diseases. There was a tribe of people who live in the jungles of the Amazon that did not want this relic to be found because it was sacred to them. That is why the assignment was such a dangerous one. After a long and treacherous journey into the deep jungle, Millie was able to locate the relic and made a deal with the tribe in exchange for them allowing her to take the relic home with her. She explained how the relic could be helpful in curing millions of people and promised to handle it with care and respect. In exchange for food and supplies, the Chief of the tribe agreed to allow Millie to take the relic. She returned home after an exhausting yet rewarding 6 months. She felt accomplished because she had successfully completed her mission and was hopeful that a cure for cancer was in the process of now being found.

_____ self-corrections _____ errors   types of miscues _____ (m) _____ (s) _____ (v)

Observations: Possible comprehension questions;

1) What was Millie's mission?

2) Why was it dangerous for her to be in the jungle?

The Storm Chaser

Written by Lisa Brashier
227 words, 3rd grade
student Version

Kate Franklin had always dreamed of being a storm chaser from the time she was a little girl. She had always been obsessed with watching thunderstorms. She was fascinated with how weather worked. Anytime there was a warning issued for a thunderstorm or a tornado, she would get excited. This is something that a lot of people don't understand because of the dangerous nature of bad weather; however, this never mattered to Kate. She would go outside to observe everything that was happening and would take notes of the clouds and wind. As she grew older, she decided that she wanted to go to college for meteorology. After graduating, she decided to fulfill her lifelong dream of chasing storms and tornadoes. She planned her trip to Oklahoma around peak tornado season and was prepared to leave when a terrible yet beautiful storm rolled in to her hometown. She immediately took action in gathering her equipment and set out to find the best location to film the storm as it made its way through town. The storm ended up producing a tornado that tore a huge path through the town. No one was injured or killed, thankfully, but Kate was able to get some beautiful pictures and videos of the tornado itself. It was a wonderful start to her new journey as a meteorologist and a storm chaser.

© solarseven/Shutterstock.com

The Storm Chaser

Written by Lisa Brashier
227 words, 3rd grade
Teacher Version

Kate Franklin had always dreamed of being a storm chaser from the time she was a little girl. She had always been obsessed with watching thunderstorms. She was fascinated with how weather worked. Anytime there was a warning issued for a thunderstorm or a tornado, she would get excited. This is something that a lot of people don't understand because of the dangerous nature of bad weather; however, this never mattered to Kate. She would go outside to observe everything that was happening and would take notes of the clouds and wind. As she grew older, she decided that she wanted to go to college for Meteorology. After graduating, she decided to fulfill her lifelong dream of chasing storms and tornadoes. She planned her trip to Oklahoma around peak tornado season and was prepared to leave when a terrible, yet beautiful, storm rolled in to her hometown. She immediately took action in gathering her equipment and set out to find the best location to film the storm as it made its way through town. The storm ended up producing a tornado that tore a huge path through the town. No one was injured or killed, thankfully, but Kate was able to get some beautiful pictures and videos of the tornado itself. It was a wonderful start to her new journey as a meteorologist and a storm chaser.

_____ self-corrections _____ errors   types of miscues _____ (m) _____ (s) _____ (v)

Observations: Possible comprehension questions:

1) Why do you think Kate wanted to be a storm chaser?

2) Why is that a dangerous job?

The Walk Home

Written by Tara Wilson
145 words, 2nd grade
Student Version

One afternoon, on her way home from school, Kim fell down and hurt her leg. Her leg was scraped up real bad and bleeding! She sat on the sidewalk until someone came along. Mr. Ruiz, the PE teacher from her school stopped when he saw Kim sitting on the sidewalk crying.

Kim asked Mr. Ruiz, "Can you help me?"

"Yes, I do not think your leg is too bad. We need to clean it before we do anything else," Mr. Ruiz responded.

"Will cleaning it hurt?" said Kim.

Mr. Ruiz shook his head no, as he pulled a bottle of water and a rag out of his backpack. Mr. Ruiz pour some water onto her leg and then carefully washed it off. Kim felt better. Mr. Ruiz walked with Kim until she safely got to her home.

"Thank you! You are the best!" said Kim.

© Kastoluza/Shutterstock.com

The Walk Home

Written by Tara Wilson
145 words, 2nd grade
Teacher Version

One afternoon, on her way home from school, Kim fell down and hurt her leg. Her leg was scraped up real

bad and bleeding! She sat on the sidewalk until someone came along. Mr. Ruiz, the PE teacher from her school

stopped when he saw Kim sitting on the sidewalk crying.

Kim asked Mr. Ruiz, "Can you help me?"

"Yes, I do not think your leg is too bad. We need to clean it before we do anything else," Mr. Ruiz responded.

"Will cleaning it hurt?" said Kim.

Mr. Ruiz shook his head no, as he pulled a bottle of water and a rag out of his backpack. Mr. Ruiz pour some

water onto her leg and then carefully washed it off. Kim felt better. Mr. Ruiz walked with Kim until she safely

got to her home.

"Thank you! You are the best!" said Kim.

_____ self-corrections _____ errors   types of miscues _____ (m) _____ (s) _____ (v)

Observations: Possible comprehension question: Why did Mr. Ruiz help Kim?

Tiny

Written by Tara Wilson
156 words, 2nd grade
Student Version

Long ago big, strong horses were important to farmers. Farmers depended on the big horses. It was no surprise, then, when Jacob's dad was extremely mad the day Jacob came home from town.

Farmer Smith, Jacob's dad, had told him to go into town to collect money a man owed him. However, Jacob did not return with the money but a small horse. The gossip was already spreading that Farmer Smith had a tiny, new horse. People were laughing! What good was a tiny horse when there is a lot of work to do on a farm?

Jacob told his dad about the tiny horse's strength, hoping he would not be mad anymore. Farmer Smith did not listen. He punched the wall, yelling at Jacob. The tiny horse had to go!

The next morning Farmer Smith took Jacob and his son to town to get his money and to return the horse. Now, Jacob was upset.

© Nynke van Holten/Shutterstock.com

Tiny

Written by Tara Wilson
156 words, 2nd grade
Teacher Version

Long ago big, strong horses were important to farmers. Farmers depended on the big horses. It was no sur-

prise, then, when Jacob's dad was extremely mad the day Jacob came home from town.

Farmer Smith, Jacob's dad, had told him to go into town to collect money a man owed him. However, Jacob

did not return with the money, but a small horse. The gossip was already spreading that Farmer Smith had a

tiny, new horse. People were laughing! What good was a tiny horse when there is a lot of work to do on a farm?

Jacob told his dad about the tiny horse's strength, hoping he would not be mad anymore. Farmer Smith did

not listen. He punched the wall, yelling at Jacob. The tiny horse had to go!

The next morning Farmer Smith took Jacob and his son to town to get his money and to return the horse.

Now, Jacob was upset.

_____ self-corrections _____ errors   types of miscues _____ (m) _____ (s) _____ (v)

Observations: Possible comprehension question: Why was Farmer Smith mad?

Reading Difficulties

Source: Tara Wilson

When to worry about whether a student has an issue with reading does not always have a clear-cut answer. Teachers and parents have the tendency to compare two students. This is especially true when there is an older sibling who did not struggle with reading and who just kind of "breezed" through the process. Thus, it is important to note that students may have weaknesses that need to be addressed or that reading has not yet "clicked." In this section, you will learn about reading weaknesses and how to know if students just are not ready. A brief discussion on dyslexia is provided as well.

Weaknesses

Some students struggle with *decoding* words, even when the word is phonetically accurate. The student may omit or add sounds. For example, they read dream for deem. In a seminal study, Stanovich (1986) discovered that early difficulties in phonological awareness underlie later reading issues. Students who do not think of the last sound of cat as /t/ will not be able to use the letter t to correctly identify the word. Their decoding skills are very laborious and slow.

Students can also have issues with *text structures*. The way information is organized in a text is referred to as text structures. They can impact reading comprehension, especially with non-fiction text (Reutzel & Cooter, 2019). This issue can occur when decoding is takes a lot of effort, rendering students unable to assimilate information into a coherent whole, or when students do not understand how to distinguish the overall structure of a text. Either way, students who struggle with text structures benefit from specific instruction on this issue. Reutzel and Cooter (2019) posit that "effective text structure instruction requires that teachers provide short, frequent review opportunities for application of the text structure stratgies taught" (p 272). One possible strategy for teaching text structure is to create an anchor chart and then have students go on a scavenger hunt. A word of caution, though. It is not enough for students to just simply make observations but they need to be able to explain the purpose of why the text is structured in a particular way.

Studying high-frequency *sight words* is a common practice in the early grades. High-frequency sight words are words that appear most often in text and must be recognized automatically. This is because some common words in the English language do not follow the "rules" (i.e., have and eye) A student might guess a lot or try to sound out these common words.

The student may sound out words, but they cannot put them all together on the page in a coherent manner. This is a problem because several high-frequency words cannot be easily decoded using phonics skills (Reutzel & Cooter, 2019). The reading is choppy. *Fluency* could very well be is the issue. Fluency is the ability to read with speed, accuracy and with appropriate prosody. A fluent reader decodes effortlessly and accurately while simultaneously comprehending what is being read. If a student is not a fluent reader, then their comprehension can be affected. Comprehension is the main goal of reading. Please note that fluency gradually develops through practice. Thus, kindergarten and first grade teachers should not worry too much if a student is a fluent reader or not. During the early stages of reading, students are still learning what reading is and how to read. They are learning what letters are, attaching sounds to letters, and blending sounds into real words.

Not "Clicked" Yet

Not all students progress through the reading process at the same rate. Some need more time than others. Students come from all backgrounds; several belong to families that read daily, while others do not have any books in their home. Findings from Stanovich's seminal study (1986) noted that several of the problems striving readers have are not due to underlying causes but due to students' lack of reading experiences. Getting books into every home is of utmost importance!

Research has proven that having books in the home positively effects a child in a plethora of ways. One such study conducted by Sikora, Evans & Kelley (2019) found that the mer presence of books in the home enhances a child's educational achievement, attainment and even their future occupational standings.

However, some students who do come from homes where reading is prominent still can have delayed reading processes—reading simply does not interest them. Motivation can be a factor for students who seem to struggle with reading. A student might not be motivated to read for many reasons, including not challenging, lack of meaning, attention seeking, and fear of failure. To increase a student's motivation, you can model a daily love of reading; provide a safe, accepting literacy environment; allow students to choose what they read; and relate to their interest whenever possible.

What are some *specific* examples of how a teacher can motivate students to read?

Elaborate on the reasons why a student might not be motivated to read.

What it is	What it is not
Language-based learning disability associated with reading	Simply reading letters or words backwards
Brain is wired differently	Laziness
Many with dyslexia are intelligent	Low level of IQ
Accommodations and strategies available for success	Curable disease

Some space is intentionally left blank so that you can add to the table.

Dyslexia

When a student struggles with reading, the first word that comes to mind is "dyslexia." Dyslexia is an issue but might not be the reason why a student is struggling with reading. . It is important for everyone, especially teachers, to know what dyslexia is and is not.

Dyslexia is defined by the International Dyslexia Association (2006) as a "specific learning disability, neurological in origin, that is characterized by difficulties with accurate and / or fluent word recognition and by poor spelling and decoding abilities. These difficulties typically result from a deficit in the phonological component of language that is often unexpected in relation to other cognitive abilities an the level of effective classroom instruction provided. Secondary consequences may include problems in reading comprehension and reduced reading engagement that can impede growth of vocabulary and background knowledge"

Dyslexia experts suggest that instruction for students with dyslexia be intensive, multi-sensory and individualized. Not all students with dyslexia are alike, so it is important to provide instruction that is aligned with the particular student's specific learning needs / goals.

Also refer to the *Books to Check Out* page in the resource section of your workbook for books on dyslexia.

Review

What do you feel are three big takeaways from this section?

1.

2.

3.

Thoughts to Ponder

Reflect on each of the following statements and questions. Write your reflection in the space provided. Then discuss your thoughts with a partner.

Do you think students know that the main goal of reading is to comprehend text? Why, or why not?

Should you worry if a 3rd grader has issues with decoding? Why, or why not?

What comes to your mind when you hear the word dyslexia?

What role does motivation play in reading?

Assignment: Interview an elementary aged student to uncover their feelings about reading.

Resources

Questions to Ask Yourself When Assessing a Student

Automatic Word Recognition

What level of material should be used for the student's instruction?

How often does the student self-correct?

Does the student use context to go with subpar decoding skills?

Are words read better in isolation or in context?

Can the student decode words in context that they cannot decode in isolation or vice versa?

Is the student familiar with any spelling patterns? If so, which ones?

What is the student's level of phonemic awareness?

How often does the student pause to sound out words? Are the pauses excessive?

Is the student's "sight word" knowledge adequate? How about the same for high-frequency words?

Does the child have adequate "sight word" knowledge?

How familiar is the student with the given topic?

Space to write your own automatic word recognition questions.

Fluency

Can the student read naturally and fluently, not like a robot? (or)

Does the student halt often?

Is the student fluent in context?

How often does the student skip words while reading?

Space to write your own fluency questions.

Language Comprehension

Remember:

*Teachers can determine if a student has an issue with comprehension. That is not enough, though. Teachers must ask why.

*On a daily basis, teachers will encounter students that can read fluently but unfortunately do not understand what they read.

*Knowledge of word meanings is the best predictor of comprehension. This applies to both selections containing a set of words which the student knows meanings for and selections in general.

When reading silently, at what level can the student comprehend? What is the level of comprehension when reading aloud?

Can the student comprehend what they accurately read?

When listening to a reading-aloud session (on their level), does the student comprehend?

Does the student have an acceptable vocabulary for understanding?

What kinds of questions give the student the most trouble?

Does the student use story structure to assist them with comprehension?

Does the student use common text and sentence structure to help them with comprehension?

Does the student have a suitable background knowledge? If not, what do they do?

If the student has poor decoding skills, is their comprehension hindered?

What is hindering their comprehension: limited prior knowledge, vocabulary, undeveloped strategies, or something else.

Considering the student's age and grade level, is their vocabulary adequate?

How long does it take for the student to comprehend the text?

Space to write your own language comprehension questions.

Miscues

Does the student know which errors need fixing?

Does the student choose a substitution that makes sense in the selection or sentence? (This is in reference to a meaning error.)

Does the student repeat any phrases excessively?

Does the student self-correct excessively?

Is the student's knowledge of decoding strategies sufficient?

Does the student's reading sound like language that follows a grammatical form? (this is referring to a structure error)

Does the student follow the text structure? (this is referring to a structure error)

Does the student say a word that has graphic similarity to the word in the selection? (This is in reference to a visual error.)

What curing systems, if any, does the student use to correct errors? (This is in reference to self-correction.)

Does the student's errors show that they are reading for meaning or just sounding out the words?

Is the student limited to saying the first sound and then making a guess, or does the student know to extend their scanning to the entire word and chunk? (when appropriate)

Does the student get nervous when being assessed?

Space to write your own miscue questions.

Strategic Control

What is the student's knowledge of print concepts?

Does the student use different strategies during reading?

Does the student use a set of strategies to achieve different purposes for reading?

How often is a student using strategies while reading?

What type of strategies are they using?

Space to write your own strategic control questions.

Other

Can the student describe the purposes for reading?

Does the student have a positive attitude or a negative attitude toward reading? Why is that?

According to the student, what is the goal of reading?

What is the student's favorite genre? Do they have one?

Space to write your own other questions.

People to Know

Throughout your study of literacy, especially on reading assessments, you will come across a myriad of literacy experts. Given here is a recommendation of a select few "gurus" that are worth getting to know. Space is provided for you to add people who you feel are worth noting.

Betts, Emmett (1903 to 1987)

Emmett Betts was a pioneer in reading. He used his psychological background to develop the Betts Ready to Read test. This assessment determines a young student's preparedness to read. Dr. Betts stressed the importance of laboratory demonstrations and having a clinical approach to reading instruction while highlighting the psychology behind reading processes.

Dr. Betts is famous for his perseverance on the necessity for tailoring reading instruction to the needs and the reading levels of students. However, Dr. Betts most known achievement are informal reading inventories. He developed these inventories to instruct classroom teachers to be perceptive about reading behaviors of their students.

Dr. Betts was a driving force in organizing the International Council for the Improvement of Reading Instruction, which later evolved into the International Reading Association. Today, this organization is known as the International Literacy Association.

Books (not an all-inclusive list):

Prevention and Correction of Reading Difficulties (1938)
Visual Problems of School Children (1941)
Discovering Specific Reading Needs (1943)
Foundations of Reading Instruction (1957)

Source: readinghalloffame.org/Emmett-betts

Calkins, Lucy

Lucy Calkins, or just Lucy, is a household, or rather "schoolhold," name. Her name is bound to be mentioned when talking about reading or writing. Many schools across the United States have adopted her Units of Study program.

Lucy established the infamous Teacher's College Reading and Writing Project. This project has existed for more than 30 years, influencing literacy instruction worldwide.

Currently, Lucy is a professor of Children's Literature at Columbia University. At Columbia she codirects a literacy specialist program.

Books (not an all-inclusive list):

Living Between the Lines (1991)
The Art of Teaching Reading (2000)
Reading Pathways, Performance Assessments & Learning Progressions (2015)
Leading Well: Building Schoolwide Excellence in Reading and Writing (2018)

Source: Heinemann.com/authors/430aspx

Chall, Jeanne (1921 to 1999)

Jeanne Chall was another reading pioneer. During her professional life she studied many topics, but the most prominent ones were readability, vocabulary, reading development, and beginning reading methods. Out of her studies came several publications, literacy assessments, and, most notably, her stages of reading development.

Chall's six stages of reading development has provided a blueprint for reading development. A child starts in pre-reading (becoming aware of print) and ends with advanced literacy activity (e.g., assimilating material for a master's course). She was one of the first literacy researchers to call reading a developmental process.

During her tenure as a Harvard professor, Chall worked beside colleagues from different institutions to develop literacy assessments. Along with Edgar Dale, Ohio State University, she developed the Dale–Chall Readability Formula. This assessment was updated later. The original formula took about 18 pages to complete; now it takes only about two pages. Then along with Florence Roswell, City College New York, she developed the Roswell–Chall Diagnostic Reading Test of Word Analysis Skills. This test is administered individually and takes about 5 minutes per student. This test is most appropriate for any student who struggles with word recognition skills.

Books (not an all-inclusive list):

Readability: An Approach of Research and Application (1974)
Stages of Reading (1983)
The Reading Crisis: Why Poor Children Fall Behind (1990)
Creating Successful Readers: Practical Guide to Testing & Teaching At All Levels (1994)

Source: readinghallofffame.org/Jeanne-chall

Chappuis, Jan

When discussing the topic of assessments (and not just literacy assessments), Chappuis is one name that we can hardly ever miss. Jan Chappuis, an independent consultant, is an assessment guru.

Before becoming an assessment expert, Chappuis was a classroom teacher, teaching grades 4th through 9th. During her time as a teacher, she focused on getting her students engaged in their learning by using metacognitive strategies. It was through these strategies that she developed lessons that increased students' understanding of not only the content but of themselves as learners. Chappuis quickly became a supporter of using different assessments to advance, not just measure, achievement.

After Chappuis left the classroom, she became a curriculum developer, then a staff developer. Her focus shifted from students to teachers, particularly toward how teachers can utilize assessment practices that aid learning among students. Currently, Chappuis serves as a consultant and traveling across the country helps schools establish classrooms where assessment practices support efficient learning among students.

Books (not an all-inclusive list):

Seven Strategies of Assessment for Learning (2015)
Classroom Assessment for Student Learning: Doing it Right—Using it Well (2012)
An Introduction to Student Involved Assessment for Learning (2012)
Creating and Recognizing Quality Rubrics (2006)

Source: janchappuis.com

Clay, Marie (1926 to 2007)

Marie Clay, a native of New Zealand, known worldwide, even after her death, for her work in psychology (developmental and school) and in literacy. Her work has been translated in different languages. Clay is probably best known for developing Reading Recovery. The driving question behind Reading Recovery is, "What is possible when we change the design and delivery of traditional education for children that teachers find hard to teach?" (Clay, 1993).

Reading Recovery is a short-term intervention of one-to-one tutoring for elementary students who are not quite achieving at their grade level. Each tutoring session lasts about 30 minutes every school day for 12 to 20 weeks with a specially trained teacher. Once the student meets grade-level expectations, they are "released" from the program.

Marie Clay's other accomplishments are in the areas of oral language, writing, and accommodating students with special needs. Clay worked to redesign the early identification and instruction of students with special needs, not just classroom practices.

Books (not an all-inclusive list):

Becoming Literate (1991)
Reading Recovery: A guidebook for Teachers (1993)
By Different Paths to Common Outcomes (1998)
An Observation Survey of Early Literacy Development (2002)

Source: readingrecovery.org/reading-recovery/teaching-children/marie-clay/

Diller, Debbie

Debbie Diller has been in the education field since 1976. She spent several years as a classroom teacher, teaching grades from prekindergarten to sophomore year in high school. After leaving the classroom, she was a literacy coach and a reading specialist; traveling across the United States, she is now into consulting.

Diller is best known for her expertise on literacy stations. She has written several books, and she conducts online courses (for anyone interested) on realistic ways teachers can meet the literacy needs of all students.

Books (not an all-inclusive list):

Literacy Work Stations: Making Centers Work (2002)
Practice with Purpose: Literacy Stations for Grades 3–6 (2004)
Making the Most of Small Groups: Differentiation for All (2006)
Spaces and Places: Designing Classrooms for Literacy (2007)

Source: debbiediller.com

Ehri, Linnea

Many psychologists are involved in literacy research, as you might have noticed. One well-known psychologist is Dr. Linnea Ehri. Dr. Ehri's research has revolved around the following areas: language and cognitive development, psycholinguistics, and reading and spelling acquisition. Her studies have added to the understanding of the sources of difficulty and the psychological processes in learning how to spell and read.

Dr. Ehri's years of research has uncovered many important findings. Two of her major findings are that spelling effects reading and that sight words are memorized. Dr. Ehri found that a reader's conception of sounds in words is influenced by their learning to spell words. This helps students to learn and remember new vocabulary. Readers, also, use their grapheme–phoneme knowledge in order to commit sight words into their memory.

Books (not an all-inclusive list):

The Recognition of Words (1978)
Word Recognition in Beginning Literacy (1998)
Reading Acquisition (2017)

Source: https://www.gc.cuny.edu/Faculty/Core-Bios/Linnea-Ehri

Fountas and Pinnell

Dr. Irene C. Fountas (professor at Lesley University) and Dr. Gay Su Pinnell (professor at The Ohio State University) are best known as Fountas and Pinnell. They are both former classroom teachers that are now nationally known literacy field-based researchers who have written many books and created the well-known Leveled Literacy Intervention (LLI) system.

LLI is designed for intensive, highly structured, sequenced, engaging, small-group instruction. The kits include everything (take-home books, student folders, lessons, etc.) a teacher needs to conduct his or her small literacy group. Fountas and Pinnell have achieved much more in the field of literacy than LLI; they are authors of a myriad of books, articles, and teacher resources.

In Fountas and Pinnell's perspective, teacher expertise lies at the heart of student achievement. Therefore, they develop teacher friendly resources to be used as guides that teachers can often refer to as they work with readers. Both Fountas and Pinnell have a Reading Recovery (see Marie Clay above) background, which is evident in their resources that enable teachers to ground their instruction in rationales and meet the unique needs of each student.

Books (not an all-inclusive list)

Guiding Readers and Writers: Teaching Comprehension, Genre, and Content Literacy (2000)
Genre Study: Teaching with Fiction and Nonfiction Books (2012)
Guided Reading, 2nd ed. (2016)
When Readers Struggle: Teaching That Works (2017)

Source: https://www.fountasandpinnell.com/authors/

Goodman, Kenneth

Throughout this book, you have seen the name Goodman. Kenneth Goodman, a former University of Arizona professor, researched the reading process, and his major interest is miscues.

His miscue analysis serves as a diagnostic tool that provides more insight into a child's reading process. Dr. Goodman does not use the terms "mistake" or "error" because those two words implicate value (more about miscues in Section 2).

©Andrey Bespalow/shutterstock.com

Books (not an all-inclusive list):

Phonics Phacts (1993)
On the Revolution of Reading (2003)
The Truth About Dibels: What it is—What it does (2005)
Reading—The Grand Illusion: How and Why People Make Sense of Print (2016)

Source: https://www.readinghalloffame.org/ken_goodman

Harvey, Stephanie

As you assess students on their reading abilities, you will notice that some students struggle with comprehension. Stephanie Harvey is a consultant you can turn to for help on comprehension strategies. Harvey has created The Comprehension Toolkit series. Each toolkit is geared toward a cluster of different grade levels. Included in each toolkit are a plethora of lessons and explicit frameworks for teaching comprehension. Teachers are given some freedom to design or tweak the lessons to meet the specific needs of their students.

Harvey has more than a decade of public-school teaching experience, both in general and special education. She has always been curious about student

©Evgeny Atamanenko/shutterstock.com

thinking. One of her main beliefs is that schools should be a safe place for deep thought, curiosity, and inquiry. Harvey's beliefs stem from her research in comprehension, inquiry-based learning, content area literacy, non-fiction, engagement, and the role of wonder in learning.

Currently, Harvey offers presentations, coaching sessions, keynote speeches, workshops, ongoing consultations, and demonstration lessons for all types of literacy leaders nationwide.

Books (not an all-inclusive list):

Nonfiction Matters: Reading, Writing, and Research Grades 3–8 (1998)
From Striving to Thriving: How to Grow Confident, Capable Readers (2017)
Strategies that Work (3rd ed.): Teaching Comprehension for Engagement, Understanding and Building Knowledge (2017)
From Striving to Thriving Writers: Strategies the Jump Start Writing (2018)

Source: stephanieharvey.com

Stanovich, Keith

When studying reading, you will read about the Matthew Effect. Keith Stanovich, a Canadian psychologist, coined the term to describe what happens when a student struggles at the early stages of reading. They often dislike reading; thus, they read less and less than their peers who are stronger readers, true to the adage, "The rich get richer, while the poor get poorer." Stanovich is one of the 50 most cited developmental psychologists because of his research on the Matthew Effect.

©screensolutions gmbh/shutterstock.com

Stanovich was inducted into the reading hall of fame in 1995. His research in reading has been fundamental in the scientific consensus about what reading is, how it works, and what it does to the brain.

Books (not an all-inclusive list):

Progress in Understanding Reading: Scientific Foundations and New Frontiers (2000)
What Intelligence Test Miss: The Psychology of Rational Thought (2010)
Rationality and the Reflective Mind (2010)
How to Think Straight About Psychology (10th ed.) (2012)

Source: https://www.readinghalloffame.org/Keith_Stanovich

Research a literacy leader not mentioned in Section 5.

Data Binders

Data binders are a great way for students to own their learning! Any student, regardless of grade level, can maintain a data binder. Here is the what, why, when, and how of data binders.

What: three ring binders where students, teachers, administrators, and parents keep track of individual student performance. Each student is able to take ownership of their learning by setting specific goals and use their data to determine or see the progress toward their goals.

Why: Most students like to know where they stand. They often assess their achievements and act on inferences drawn about themselves. Data binders allow students to keep up with their learning on a personal level.

When: to improve academic and/or behavioral performance; for motivation; to establish ownership in learning and to teach goal setting.

How: First, a teacher models how to goal set and collect data by using a classroom goal. When students are comfortable with the classroom example, then it is time for them to set individual goals. Tip: Start off with concrete data (like numbers of items correct)

Some ideas (geared toward literacy): fluency rates, reading levels, letter–sound correspondence, spelling tests, number of books read, any type of grade tracking, and word wall words.

©sasirin pamai/shutterstock.com

Books to Check Out

Comprehension

Hoyt, L. (2008). *Revisit, reflect, retell: Time-tested strategies for teaching reading comprehension*. Portsmouth, NH: Heinemann.

Stahl, K., & Garcia, G. (2015). *Developing reading comprehension: Effective instruction for all students in prek-2*. New York, NY: The Guilford Press.

Dyslexia

Brock, L., & Eide, M. (2012). *The dyslexic advantage: Unlocking the hidden potential of the dyslexic brain*. London, England: Plume.

Shaywitz, S. (2005). *Overcoming dyslexia*. New York, NY: Vintage.

IRIs

Johns, J. (2012). *Basic reading inventory* (11th ed.). Dubuque, IA: Kendall-Hunt.

Leslie, L., & Caldwell, J. (2010). *Qualitative reading inventory-5*. Upper Saddle River, NJ: Pearson.

Woods, M.L., & Moe, A.J. (2010). *Analytical reading inventory* (9th ed.). Upper Saddle River, NJ: Pearson.

Reading (in general)

Harvey, S., & Ward, A. (2017). *From striving to thriving: How to grow confident, capable, readers*. New York, NY: Scholastic.

Miller, D. (2009). *The book whisper: Awakening the inner reader in every child*. San Francisco, CA: Jossey-Bass.

Miller, D. (2012). *Reading with meaning: Teaching comprehension in the primary grades* (2nd ed.). Portsmouth, NH: Stenhouse.

Miller, D., & Kelley, S. (2013). *Reading in the wind: The book whisper's keys to cultivating lifelong reading habits*. San Francisco, CA: Jossey-Bass.

Spelling

Bear, D.R., Invernizzi, M., Templeton, S., & Johnston, F. (2020). *Words their way: Word study for phonics, vocabulary, and spelling instruction* (7th ed.). Upper Saddle River, NJ: Pearson/Prentice Hall.

*Use this space to write books that you come across:

References

Chappuis, J. & Stiggins, R. (2012). *Introduction to student-involved assessment for learning* (6th ed.) Pearson.

Clay, M. (2013). *An observation survey of early literacy achievement* (3rd ed.). Heinemann.

Clay, M. (2000). *Running records for classroom teachers*. Heinemann.

Leslie, L. & Caldwell, J. (2010). *Qualitative reading inventory* (5th ed.) Pearson.

McKenna, M. & Stahl, K. (2015). *Assessment for Reading* (3rd ed). The Guilford Press.

Reutzel, D.R. & Cooter, R.B. (2019). *Teaching children to read: The teacher makes the Difference* (8th ed.). Pearson.

Scriven, M. (1991). *Evaluation thesaurus* (4th ed.) Sage.

Sikora, J., Evans, M., & Kelley, J. (2019). Scholarly culture: How books in adolescence enhance adult literacy, numeracy and technical skills. *Social Science Research*, 77(1). 1-15.

Serravallo, J. (2018). *Understanding texts & readers: Responsive comprehension Instruction with leveled texts*. Heinemann.

Stanovich, K. (1986). Matthew effects in reading: Some consequences of individual Differences in the acquisition of literacy. *Reading Research Quarterly*, 21(4). 360-407.

Woods, M. & Moe, A. (2015). *Analytical reading inventory: Comprehensive standards based assessment for all students including gifted and remedial* (10th ed.). Pearson.